YOUR KNOWLEDGE HAS VALUE

Junaid Javaid

Digital Business Management Report on southwest.com

GRIN Verlag

Bibliografische Information der Deutschen Nationalbibliothek:

Die Deutsche Bibliothek verzeichnet diese Publikation in der Deutschen National-
bibliografie; detaillierte bibliografische Daten sind im Internet über http://dnb.d-
nb.de/ abrufbar.

Imprint:

Copyright © 2012 GRIN Verlag GmbH
Druck und Bindung: Books on Demand GmbH, Norderstedt Germany
ISBN: 978-3-656-74817-5

This book at GRIN:

http://www.grin.com/en/e-book/281114/digital-business-management-report-on-
southwest-com

Digital Business Management Report on southwest.com

Assessment-1

Submitted By:
Junaid Javaid

Date of Submission:
08/11/2012

Table of Contents

1. Introduction

This report deals with field of Digital Business Management and the chosen company for this purpose is the leader of US Low Cost Carrier (LCC) called Southwest Airline, And for completion of this report southwest.com is critically analysed. This report is composed of four section. In very first section, southwest.com is analysed in term of information systems implemented by the company. In the second section, Southwest Airline's online business model is carefully observed and analysed. Then in the third phase, Southwest Airlines e-CRM is being evaluated in identifying its customer acquisition and customer retention policy. And in forth and the last section few recommendations are made to strengthen its digital business strategy.

2. Website (southwest.com) Evaluation

With reference to the website (southwest.com) of United States no.1 Lowe Cost Carrier called Southwest Airline. It has been cleared that southwest.com is the central component in company's operations as about 70% of their tickets are sold through this platform. And no doubt in saying that the Southwest Airline's website is the combination of different information systems as It allows to perform operations like booking flights, managing flights, frequent flyer program and made them to offer complementary products and services through their business Partners. And all these operations are possible as their website is connected to different systems which are Online Flight reservation system, customer management system, flight management system and Analytics & content management system. So one can say that major portion of Southwest Airline's operations is performed through its website.

We all knew that the Airline business process depend heavily on its reservation system. So as we know that Southwest Airline has adopted Direct Sales model in order to reduce the transaction (agent) cost. And for this purpose they have implemented online reservation system offered by Sabre named as SabreSonic Res. This system uses advanced technologies which allow customers to make reservation online and thus helping Southwest Airline in making competitiveness sustained (Sabre, 2011)

The Southwest Airline online reservation system has three important which explained below:

a) Reservation Engine: It provides assistance in making online transactions with customers.

b) Inventory Engine: It helps Southwest Airline in managing flight fares, scheduling flights.

c) Departure Control System: It is responsible for making final purchase which in term of issuing boarding to the specified passenger with the unique PNR serial number.

So now, we are in a position to say that Southwest Airline website's interface connected the SabreSonic Res to perform all above interconnected operations which benefits both sides (Customers and Southwest Airline). This online reservation system can be categorized as TPS (Transaction Processing System) and DSS (Decision Support System). TPS in a sense that it allows website to enable both operations (online booking and customer transaction) which are considered to be as Southwest Airline's operation activities. DSS in a sense that it also stored Customer's information in the company's database which will be proved to be beneficial for them in formulating and implementing company's new business strategy.

Southwest.com also uses and connect with the Revenue Management System offered by IBM named as IBM AS/400 which assist company's middle management by displaying company's current performance obtained from the Reservation Engine (globalthesis.com, 2004). And this information allows company in identifying sales opportunity which will results in increasing company's revenue. So one can say this system is a type of Management Information System (MIS).

Southwest.com is also connected with another system called SalesServer which is designed by PRISM Group (Edward, 2010). This system accommodates company's executive level management as it uses advanced tools to generate graph in drill to detail format. This system is critical to the company as it will also help them in making Investment decision and this system falls in the category of Executive Support System.

We can say that Southwest.com is a website that is connected to three different kinds of Information Systems for accommodating three different management levels within a company. These systems allows Southwest Airline to make its competitive edge sustainable and allows the company to serve customers in the effective manner through the integration of company's different departments.

3. Online Business Model

Southwest Airline online business model comprises of four important aspects which are listed and explained below (Markides, 2000):

- Product Innovation: It focused on the types of products and services Southwest Airline is offering to their customers.
- Financials: How much and how Southwest Airline is earning.
- Infrastructure Management: It focused on the Southwest Airline's value configuration system.
- E-Customer Relationship Management: It emphasis on the type of customers Southwest Airline is targeting.

In this section first three aspects are briefly discussed while the e-CRM will be discussed in the later section.

3.1.   Product Innovation

This factor will inclined on the company's offerings (Products & Services).

Target Customer Segment

As we knew that the Southwest Airline is a Low Cost Carrier company so the customers they are targeting are those who are price conscious.

3.1.1.   Online Value Proposition

Southwest Airline Online Value Proposition is expressed by its Founders:

"More than 38 years ago, Rollin King and Herb Kelleher got together and decided to start a different kind of airline. They began with one simple notion: If you get your passengers to their destinations when they want to get there, on time, at the lowest possible fares, and make darn sure they have a good time doing it, people will fly your airline."

3.1.2.   Capability

The Capability factor emphasize on the ability of the company in utilising its assets in generating sales for the company and also which results in superior customer services. It has been observed and analysed that the Southwest Airline is very effective and efficient in utilizing its assets.

3.2.   Financials

3.2.1.   Online Revenue Model

a) Direct Selling: About 70% of Southwest Airline sales takes place through its website. Sp it is being cleared that Southwest Airline relied mostly on direct selling which cut short the agent cost thus making Southwest Airline to align its Revenue building policies with its business strategy.

b) Affiliate Model: Southwest Airline Vacation affiliate program is the prominent factor in this regards as Southwest Airline charging commission from its partners through the online offering of conventional products (Hotel Reservation & Car Rental) and is prove to be as the second biggest source of Southwest Airline in revenue generation.

c) Advertising: This is least factor in Southwest Airline online revenue generation. And Southwest.com generates online revenue by selling advertising space to other willing companies for the purpose of enhancing their partners product or service (offerings) awareness.

3.3.   Infrastructure Management

This aspect will focus on the Southwest Airline's value configuration system which not only helps Southwest Airline in delivering its products or services in a best specific manner but also helps them in acquiring and retaining their customer range through Customer Relationship Management.

3,3,1, Resources

This factor deals with the types of resources the company have had in creating and enhacing the value of the firm. For this purpose Southwest Airline has top three resources which are listed below:

   i.   Employees (Explicit Knowledge)
  ii.   Southwest.com (Implicit Knowledge)
 iii.   Boeing 737 (Explicit Knowledge)

3.3.2. Activity Configuration

This factor deals with value creating aspects of the company for which customers are willing to pay. This reflects to the company's primary activities and support activities its business processes known as Value Chain. Southwest Airline three value creating aspects are listed below:

- Southwest Airline Service Provisioning
- Southwest Airline Networks Promotions and Contract Management
- Southwest Airline Infrastructural Operations

3.3.3. Partner Network

This factor focused towards the company's activity configuration distributed among its business partners. This activity configuration not only resulting in reducing the overall transaction cost but also makes the company to oppose the threat of vertical integration. In this regards Southwest Airline has made strong affiliation with its business partner which are the Second Airport and the control system of US Air Traffic.

So the crocks of all three aspects explained above is that Southwest Airline is successful in harnessing and implementing its online business model in a best possible manner and that is why it is the leader in US Low Cost Carrier Industry. In term of its product innovation, Southwest Airline is aggressive in managing its infrastructure. Southwest Airline is also successful in aligning its business through the direct selling of Air tickets and at the lowest cost. In the field of Infrastructure Southwest Airline is prove to be as the no frill Airline and also achieving its value proposition through on time flights. Thus we can say that Southwest Airline's product innovation and Infrastructure management are prominent factors in building strong relationship with their customers and thus making Southwest Airline as the value creating Brand.

4. Website's Customer Relationship Management (e-CRM)

Website CRM is mainly comprise of three components which are Information Strategy, Feel & Serve and Trust and Loyalty.

In Southwest Airline, CRM is the promising factor as their business is relied mostly on its website for the purpose of direct selling. So we can say that at this point that Southwest Airline's product innovation and superior customer service are the result of repeated sales from its available customer base and thus is the Revenue generating aspect the company.

4.1.   Information Strategy

This component focused on the gathering of customer information which results in creating and maintaining strong relationships with their customers. And all this made possible through Data Warehousing and Data Mining aspect. Southwest.com has successfully implemented PolyVista Discovery business intelligence for the purpose of Data Warehousing and Data Mining, This software enables Southwest Airline to extract through its existing customer base which helps them in making their database. Through this aspect Southwest Airline has the opportunity to design and reinvent its policies related to customer acquisition and customer retention. This software has also one more value added features called Web Analytics which Southwest Airline is to learn about their customer interaction on southwest.com. This feature helps Southwest Airline in giving idea on its websites prime location and also helps them in their website improvement or advancement. So in this manner, Southwest Airline optimising its online marketing mix by analysing the behaviour of their available customer-base.

4.2.   Distribution Channel

This component deals with the distribution channel used in creating sale of the company's offerings (products & servies). We already familiar with the concept that Southwest Airline is participating aggressively in Customer Centric E-Business (CCEB) industy, so we can say that Southwest Airline depends heavily on its website for the purpose of Distribution as about 70% of its sales are made through southwest.com while the remaining 30% are made through agents. So at this point, we can say that Southwest Airline's Direct sales model made them to utilize and use its website as the primary channel in generating sales for the company which thus results in revenue stream.

4.3.   Trust & Loyalty

This component focused more on the aspects that result in creating the customers trust and thus making their customer loyal. So one can make point at this situation that customer trust & loyal is the source of maintaining the current customer base but also results in repeated sales from the customer. Southwest Airline's customer loyalty program is the superior factors making customers loyal and thus providing value to their customer through the discount on available tickets prices.

4.4. Web Portal

Souhwest Airline in partners with VMware has implementing web portal for southwest.com which allows their member customers to use and take advantage of certain facilities like Online account balance enquiry, history of travel and transaction made with Southwest Airline, New offerings information and reward order in term of discounts or upgrades. This component is the competitive factor for Southwest Airline as it results in generating sales and also enhances their tickets liquidity via early bookings. At Southwest Airline this web portal got fame as its only help them in retaining customer but also a contributing factor in their revenue generation.

So it have been cleared that the above factors contributing equally in Southwest Airline e-CRM. That is the reason that Southwest Airline is world no.1 Airline in Low Cost Carrier and has set standards which are easy to achieve for its competitors.

5. Recommendations

Despite of so many successes Southwest Airline still needs to do some more things so as to strengthen its digital business strategy. All recommendations are listed below:

- Southwest Airline has to modify its current Customer Analytics by adding some more features which helps company in tracking customer efficient manner and also helps in customizing product offering (products & services) according to specified customer behaviour. This software should capable of sending e-mail about the new promotions to the specified customer according to their desired buying behaviour. This concept is known as Personalisation.

- Southwest Airline should introduce mobile version (mobile site) like Emirates and Qatar Airways have already introduced. This mobile site should be capable of offering all features which are normally shown on their company's website. This features not only provide customers with hand on information but making their competitiveness more sustainable.

- Southwest Airline should launch mobile portal for their member customer which enables them to enjoy all features similar to its Web Portal. So this feature not only benefits Southwest Airline's customers but to the company as well it will extra value to Southwest Airline's existing operations. This factor will prove to be loyalty enhancing component for Southwest Airline and thus results in increasing frequency of sales.

- Southwest Airline should create Fan page on popular Social Networking sites, This initiative not only benefited in advertising new routes but also give them an opportunity to offer or sell inventory at the discount rate. They can add the value creating feature on the fan page which is to offer special package to their followers in term of discounted tickets.

- Southwest Airline should requires advancement in Itinerary Functionality through the development of creative and innovative functionality. This value creating will prove to be the differentiated factor as nobody in the industry has recently offering this feature.

- Southwest Airline should introduce Online Airport Suite which is the primary source of improving Southwest Airline's online customer services.

So by following above recommendations Southwest Airline will able to make its digital business strategy more sustainable and aligned in the long-run.

6. References

Edward, T., 2010. *SalesServer.* [Online] Available at: http://webkey.prism grp.com/products/airline.asp [Accessed 10 March 2012].

globalthesis.com, 2004. *Based On Net Income Of C / S Model Management System Design And Realization.* [Online] Available at: http://www.globethesis.com/?t=2208360095460193 [Accessed 27 September 2012].

Markides, C., 2000. All the Right Moves. *Harvard Business School Press,* I(1), pp. 1-219.

Sabre, 2011. *SabreSonic Res.* [Online] Available at: http://www.sabreairlinesolutions.com/images/uploads/AS 09-11427 SS Res Component Profile FINAL.pdf [Accessed 1st October 2012].

7. Appendices

7.1.   southwest.com-Homepage

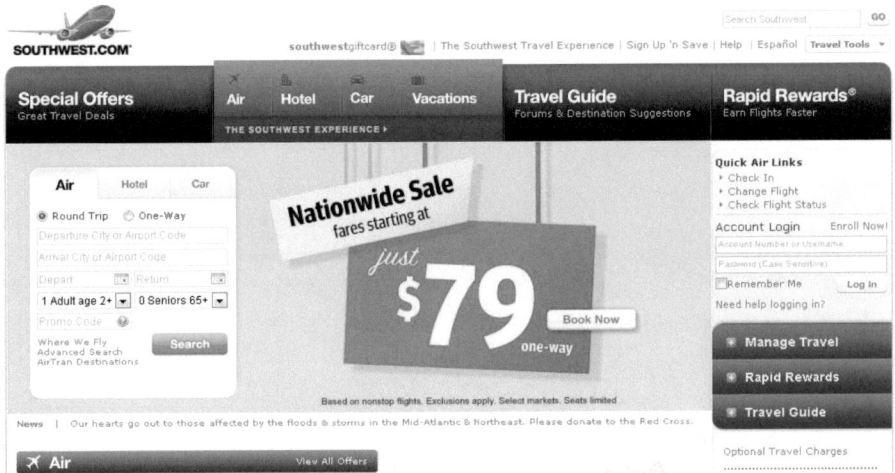